CONTENTS

WELSH
AND PROUD OF IT

CERYS JONES

summersdale

WELSH AND PROUD OF IT

Summersdale Publishers Ltd
46 West Street
Chichester
West Sussex
PO19 1RP
UK

www.summersdale.com

Printed and bound in the Czech Republic

ISBN: 978-1-84953- 524-3

Substantial discounts on bulk quantities of Summersdale books are available to corporations, professional associations and other organisations. For details contact Nicky Douglas by telephone: +44 (0) 1243 756902, fax: +44 (0) 1243 786300 or email: nicky@summersdale.com.

INTRODUCTION

From the beautiful Brecon Beacons to the exotic gardens of Portmeirion, from the infamous Mumbles pub crawl to a spot of relaxing fishing in the River Taff (be careful of those sturgeons!), this little book will take you on a tour of everything that makes Wales great.

This beautiful country is the perfect getaway location – even if you live there! So, what are you waiting for, come and join us on a magical journey through the land of song and discover what makes people Welsh… and proud of it!

MAKING HISTORY

IMPORTANT DATES IN OUR HISTORY

One of the most famous dates in Welsh folklore is when the Welsh prince, Madog ab Owain Gwynedd (Madoc to his friends), supposedly journeyed to America in **1170**. If Madoc's journey occurred (and many believe it did), it predates Christopher Columbus's famed 1492 discovery by over three hundred years. A Welshman discovering America – fancy that!

1277–1283 was a vital period in Welsh history. The bloody conquest of the country by Edward Longshanks (King Edward I of England) resulted in the annexation of the Principality of Wales and marked the end of Wales as an independent nation. Edward defeated the last prince of an independent Wales, Llywelyn ap Gruffydd, also known as Llywelyn the Last. The title of Prince of Wales is now given to the current heir apparent to the British throne.

Wales, Wales, sweet are thy
hills and vales,
Thy speech, thy song,
To thee belong,
O may they live ever in Wales.

EVAN JAMES

From 1400 to 1409, Owain Glyndŵr, the last Welshman to have been proclaimed Prince of Wales by his own people, led a long-running but ultimately unsuccessful revolt against English rule, during the reign of Henry IV. Glyndŵr remains a national hero to this day.

In 1485, Henry Tudor (Henry VII) defeated Richard III at the Battle of Bosworth. Henry was a Welshman and the involvement of Welsh soldiers at the battle played a significant part in Henry's victory. After he became king, Henry rewarded many Welshmen with government posts in London, and with important titles such as Lord Warden of the Marches.

Wales was formally united with England under the Acts of Union of **1536** and **1543** after King Henry VIII had come to distrust the lords of the Welsh counties, notwithstanding they had been placed in those positions by his father, Henry VII, in return for their support in defeating Richard III. Henry VIII's incorporation of Wales into his realm resulted in a change to the way Wales would be governed for the next few centuries. But Wales is still a proud principality and it defends its identity with passionate loyalty. And it always will!

21 December 1955 – the day Cardiff became the capital of Wales. Following a ballot of Welsh local authorities, Cardiff had soundly beaten off contenders Aberystwyth and Caernarfon thanks to its position as a major transport and industrial hub, something which had given rise to Wales becoming the world's greatest coal exporter. Though Wales did not have an official capital city before 1955, the small town of Machynlleth, in Powys, is widely considered the 'ancient capital of Wales', due to the location there of Owain Glyndŵr's parliament in 1404.

It profits a man nothing to give his soul for the whole world… but for Wales!

ROBERT BOLT

Between 1978 and 1995, the earliest human remains to have been found in Wales – dating back to 230,000 years ago – were excavated from Pontnewydd Cave, St Asaph. Bones and teeth of Neanderthal adults and children were discovered, the cave having provided a perfect shelter for the earliest form of our ancient hunter-gatherer relatives. Neanderthals are thought to have died out around 30,000–35,000 years ago.

Rugby union is the national sport of Wales and over the past century or so the nation's players have kicked and scrummed their way to eleven Grand Slam titles and twenty Triple Crowns. In **June 1999** the embodiment of Welsh sporting history was transferred from Cardiff Arms Park when the new multi-purpose, sliding-roof Millennium Stadium opened right next to it. Each year the stadium attracts over a million visitors.

Wales is a small
coat made of
deep pockets.
HORATIO CLARE

18 September 1997 will live long in the memories of all Welsh people – it was the day the country voted 'yes' on the devolution referendum, resulting in the signing of the Government of Wales Act in 1998 and the founding of the National Assembly for Wales in 1999. Wales could now write, repeal and enforce its own laws. *Pŵer i'r bobl* – power to the people!

A proud fixture in every Welsh person's
calendar is **1 March**, St David's Day.
Though sadly rejected as a bank holiday,
the day celebrates the life of the country's
most beloved son, teacher and saint.

Be joyful, and keep your faith and your creed. Do the little things that you have seen me do and heard about. I will walk the path that our fathers have trod before us.

ST DAVID

WE CAN BE HEROES

HEROES

PEOPLE WE CAN BE PROUD TO CALL OUR OWN

Welsh history is littered with alpha males running around with their tops off. But it's **Gwenllian ferch Gruffydd**, daughter of celebrated Welsh ruler Gruffydd ap Cynan, who was the country's leading warrior princess, and whose battle at Kidwelly Castle against Norman invaders lives on as the stuff of legend. Gwenllian's death during this fight also contributed to the impetus of the Great Revolt (against the same Norman invaders) of 1136. Her ghost has been known to haunt the grounds of the castle to this day.

Having survived a German torpedo attack
while on board the RMS *Lusitania* in 1915,
Margaret Mackworth became one of
Wales's leading suffragette champions
and pioneered the Representation
of the People Act 1928 – an act that
would give all women over the age
of twenty-one the right to vote.

I will go and live back in
Wales – the water I miss, and
the air; there's something
different about it.

ELLIE GOULDING

Leo Abse was much more than just a respected Welsh lawyer and politician over three decades. During the 1950s and 1960s – a period of turbulent social change in the UK – Abse was also a leading gay rights campaigner who proactively sought to decriminalise male homosexuality as well as liberalise the UK's strict divorce laws. He died in 2008, but the causes he so fervently believed in have largely been realised, with same-sex marriages having become legal in England and Wales in July 2013.

On 1 September 2013, **Gareth Bale** became the most expensive footballer on the planet. He was transferred from Tottenham Hotspur to Spanish side Real Madrid for the whopping sum of £85.3 million. That's £38,950 a day or £1,623 an hour. Not bad going for a lad from Cardiff.

This land of my fathers is dear to me
Land of poets and singers,
and people of stature
Her brave warriors, fine patriots
Shed their blood for freedom

Land! Land!
I am true to my Land!
As long as the sea serves as a wall
for this pure, dear land
May the language endure forever.

FROM 'LAND OF MY FATHERS', THE WELSH NATIONAL ANTHEM

David Lloyd George was Britain's first, and only (so far, at least!), Welsh prime minister. He led the Lloyd George Ministry – a wartime coalition government – from 1916 and stayed in the post of prime minister until 1922. As leader of Great Britain during World War One, and as one of the fathers of the modern welfare state, Lloyd George's place in Welsh – and British – history is assured. He is also the only solicitor (as opposed to barrister) to have ever been prime minister.

What is our task? To make Britain a fit country for heroes to live in.

DAVID LLOYD GEORGE

Llywelyn the Last, or Llywelyn Ein Llyw Olaf (say that five times fast!) was the last prince of an independent Wales before the country's conquest by Edward Longshanks (Edward I of England). Llywelyn died in 1282 at the Battle of Orewin Bridge at Builth Wells and his head was cut off and sent to Edward, who stuck it on a lance outside the Tower of London, where it remained for fifteen years.

Caerphilly-born Welsh Guard, **Simon Weston**, is a Welsh icon as well as a Falklands War hero. In 1982, while aboard the under-attack RFA *Sir Galahad*, Weston suffered 49 per cent burns to his body and has since had over seventy reconstructive surgeries. When Weston met Charles, Prince of Wales, after the incident, the Prince told him to 'get well soon'. 'Yes sir, I will,' was Weston's brave response.

Everything about Wales is perfect.

ELIN FFLUR

Born (1882) and raised in Rhondda, **Elizabeth Andrews** is a true Welsh groundbreaker. She was the first female organiser for the Labour Party in Wales after women were given the vote. Andrews was also a fierce social reformer and campaigner for better living and working conditions. It was Andrews's pioneering vision and campaigning that also helped open the very first nursery school in Wales, in Rhondda in 1938.

Much-loved fashion, textile and home furnishings designer Laura Mountney was born in Dowlais, Merthyr Tydfil in 1925. When Laura married Bernard, Mountney became Ashley and the rest is fashion history. In the 1960s, **Laura Ashley** gained immense popularity throughout Britain and the Ashleys' net worth soared to £60 million. Today, Laura Ashley's name proudly stands atop high street shops all over the world.

Rhodri the Great was the first, and one of only a few people in history, to be referred to as 'King of Wales'. Rhodri ap Merfyn, as he was then known, was in fact crowned king of Gwynedd – the semi-unified territories that made up north Wales – and ruled from c. AD 844 to 878.

As health minister during Prime Minister Clement Attlee's tenure, **Aneurin Bevan** – a Welsh Labour Party politician – conceived the initial foundations of the modern National Health Service. Bevan strived for a medical care service available free of charge to all Britons, as demonstrated in his most famous quote: 'No society can legitimately call itself civilised if a sick person is denied medical aid because of lack of means.'

There are so many different aspects to Wales: the language, culture, music, history and landscape. Wales is more than just a country, it's a way of life.

GARETH PRITCHARD

SOMETHING TO REMEMBER US BY

OUR NATION'S CULTURAL HIGHLIGHTS

Wales's national arena, the **Millennium Stadium**, is the third-largest sports ground in Britain and required 40,000 tonnes of concrete in its construction. Home to the nation's beloved rugby union team as well as the national football team, the building has become one of the most impressive symbols of modern Wales. The stadium can hold 74,500 fans, including the screaming variety when music icons such as Rihanna rock up to play.

WELSH stands for
Well Established Little
Shy Heroes.

TIM VINCENT

Snowdonia National Park is the country's largest national park. Jam-packed with almost every type of landscape going – a hundred lakes, 60 kilometres (37 miles) of coastline and beaches, and ninety mountain peaks, including Mount Snowdon, the tallest mountain in Wales.

I'm proud to know that despite everything the Romans, Saxons, Normans, English, Welsh gentry, cultural assimilation and industrialisation threw at us – we're still here!

DEWI PRYSOR

Wales is the 'land of castles' and while **Cardiff Castle** may be just one of many, there is nothing else quite like it. Built around 2,000 years ago (around AD 55), during the time of the Romans in Britain, the castle was continually fortified and developed over the centuries that followed, including the addition of a magnificent Norman keep.

Offa's Dyke Path is a 177-mile-long National Trail that cuts right down through the entire country, from Prestatyn in the north to Chepstow in the south. It takes about two weeks to walk the entire path but is well worth the effort – the road encompasses many of Wales's most spectacular views.

Located in Pembrokeshire, on the most westerly point of the country, **St David's Cathedral** attracts hundreds of thousands of pilgrims each year. St David's remains are buried there and for the past 1,500 years the cathedral has resounded with the voices of millions of worshippers.

Be honourable yourself
if you wish to associate
with honourable people.

WELSH PROVERB

Completed in 1805, the **Pontcysyllte Aqueduct** towers 38 metres (126 feet) above the River Dee and is a 200-year-old engineering masterpiece, not to mention a World Heritage Site. Take a ride on a narrowboat and drink in some of Wales's most dramatic views.

The annual literary festival held every May in the town of **Hay-on-Wye** (on the Welsh side of the Wales–England border) is a world-renowned celebration of books, authors and ideas. Bill Clinton once described it as 'the Woodstock of the mind'. There are over thirty bookshops dotted around the town centre, and together they are able to cater for just about any peculiar or rare reading requests you may have!

With over four million visitors a year,
South Wales's majestic mountain range
and national park, the **Brecon Beacons**,
is a place of outstanding natural beauty
– even if you have to experience Wales's
famous rainfall while you're there. Pen
y Fan is the highest peak at 886 metres
(2,907 feet) above sea level. Well worth
the climb – but take waterproofs!

Barry Island is the fun-tastic, sandy-beached paradise of South Wales. The island epitomises all that's great about traditional Welsh family holidays and has everything you could possibly need. If you fancy a trip down memory lane to when family fun meant creaky fairground rides, 10p amusement arcades, damp holiday camps, soggy fish and chips and freezing-cold walks along a battered promenade, then Barry Island is the place to be!

Over so many years and through so many difficulties, we have always managed to keep our identity and been able to welcome others.

CARWYN JONES

STARS IN OUR EYES

THE ENTERTAINERS WE LOVE

Ian Woosnam, best known to the golfing world as 'Woosie', is a much-loved golf champion who often brought home the bacon in the form of European Tour wins, but he also won twice on the USPGA Tour and became the first golfer representing Wales to win a major championship when he won the Masters in 1991. Born in Oswestry, 'Woosie' won over fifty tournaments in all in his much-celebrated career and helped make Europe competitive in the Ryder Cup.

Born in Haverfordwest in 1974, **Christian Bale** is responsible for bringing two well-known characters, Patrick Bateman *(American Pyscho)* and Batman, to life on the big screen. His most celebrated role as Batman in the *Dark Knight* trilogy was the first time a non-American actor had played this traditionally American character.

I love Wales because it's passionate, spirited and will always be my home.

JOANNA PAGE

A Welsh footballing superstar, and one of the most spectacular and successful players in the Premier League, **Ryan Giggs** has enjoyed a career never likely to be equalled, playing solely – and loyally – for Manchester United for more than two decades. For the London 2012 Olympics, Giggs was Team GB's captain. He has also captained his first love, the Wales national team, for whom he played sixty-four times.

Singing is in the Welsh blood. That's just
the way it is. And nobody has done it better
than Tiger Bay girl **Shirley Bassey**. Having
sung three (can you name which?) of
the James Bond franchise's best opening
songs, Bassey is renowned for her large,
brassy voice and is the UK's best-selling
female recording artist of all time, having
sold over 150 million records! All together
now, 'Diamonds are foreverrrrrrrrrrrrrrr.'

Many of us remember **Catherine Zeta-Jones**'s star turn as Mariette Larkin in the 1990s TV show *The Darling Buds Of May*. Of course, you may also remember her as a Hollywood superstar in the blockbusters *The Mask of Zorro*, *Traffic* and *Ocean's Twelve*. As well as being a fantastic actress, Zeta-Jones is a celebrated dancer and singer. At the age of twelve, she won a British tap dancing championship, developing skills that were to come in handy for her starring role in the hit 2002 film musical *Chicago*.

I grew up in a small fishing village on the coast of Wales. The people there have a different attitude to life than those in Hollywood – people stick together more.

CATHERINE ZETA-JONES

Acclaimed Shakespearean actor, Hollywood icon and handsome husband (twice!) of Elizabeth Taylor, **Richard Burton** was born in Pontrhydyfen in 1925. Nominated for an Oscar seven times but never winning, Burton – at the peak of his fame – was the highest-paid actor in the business. One of his most enduring roles was opposite Clint Eastwood in the excellent war movie *Where Eagles Dare* (1968).

In 1991 Port Talbot boy **Anthony Hopkins** won an Oscar for his portrayal of Hannibal Lecter in the blockbuster thriller *The Silence of the Lambs* – the only actor to ever win the award for playing a cannibal! Considered to be one of the greatest living actors, Hopkins was knighted by the Queen in 1993.

I would like to go back to Wales. I'm obsessed with my childhood and at least three times a week dream I am back there.

ANTHONY HOPKINS

Swansea singer **Bonnie Tyler** had a series of international hits in the 1980s, from the anthemic 'Total Eclipse of the Heart' to the epic 'Holding Out for a Hero'. With those two of Tyler's songs appearing regularly in lists of best-selling songs of all time, her reputation as 'International First Lady of Rock' is assured forever.

Sir Thomas John Woodward of Pontypridd is also known by another name – **Tom Jones**. With over a hundred million record sales to date, his most famous hits include the belters 'It's Not Unusual' and 'What's New Pussycat?'. Jones is also a proud Welshman, forever celebrating the place he calls home: 'I've travelled the world singing and entertaining, bringing a bit of Wales and Great Britain to my friends, colleagues and audiences. I wear my nationality on my sleeve and I'm proud of it!'

I carry Wales around inside
me. I never really left.

TOM JONES

Cardiff-born songwriter **Ivor Novello** (1893–1951) composed many popular songs and is also regarded as one of the most popular British entertainers of the twentieth century. His legacy these days can be seen in the prestigious annual Ivor Novello Awards, which celebrate the best of British songwriting and composing.

A real Welshman
will admire
Miss World for
her politics.

GREN JONES

As one-sixth of acclaimed comedy troupe Monty Python, **Terry Jones** is a living Welsh legend. Jones was the co-writer and director of the Pythons' controversial second movie, *Life of Brian* (1979), regularly voted as the greatest comedy film ever made. In March 1993, along with the other members of Monty Python, Jones had an asteroid named after him – 9622 Terryjones – located in the asteroid belt between Mars and Jupiter.

There is a certain darkness, a lyrical darkness, in the Welsh character and that is very good for creating art.

ROB BRYDON

THE WRITE STUFF

FAMOUS WRITERS, POETS AND PLAYWRIGHTS

The *Mabinogion* is a famous collection of eleven stories written in prose, collated from medieval Welsh manuscripts. The tales detail pre-Christian Celtic mythology and early medieval historical traditions. In the nineteenth century, **Lady Charlotte Guest** (an important figure in Welsh language and literature) was the first to publish English translations of the tales and thereby helped spread the word of *Mabinogion*.

Losing my Welsh temper meant gaining my Welsh accent.

EMLYN WILLIAMS

Roald Dahl, born in Llandaff, caught the hearts and imaginations of adults and children alike. But even for a creative genius, sometimes writing didn't come easy. In fact, on finishing *Matilda* he decided that it just wasn't good enough and ended up writing the whole story again. Who says practice doesn't make perfect?

Russell T. Davies's revival of the BBC's
Doctor Who in 2005 not only added depth
to the much-loved Time Lord, but also
made the Doctor more popular than he'd
ever been. Davies's first foray into television
writing was with the acclaimed show
Queer As Folk in 1999.

The Welsh are
not meant to go
out in the sun.
They start to
photosynthesise.

RHYS IFANS

The always articulate and never-mumbling
Ian Hislop, star and team captain on
Have I Got News For You, and renowned
journalist and editor of infamous political-
satirical magazine *Private Eye*, was
ironically born in Mumbles, Swansea.

One of Wales's most famous sons, **Dylan Thomas** was born in Swansea in 1914. Thomas's poems and short stories are famed for their verbal imagery and evocation of nature. His most celebrated works are the radio drama *Under Milk Wood* (later developed as a stage play and film), and the poem 'Do not go gentle into that good night'. American singer Robert Zimmerman admired this Welshman so much he changed his name to match – he became Bob Dylan.

Renowned philosopher, humanitarian and winner of the Nobel Prize in Literature (in 1950), Welshman **Bertrand Russell** was also widely known for his altercations with the British government – he was imprisoned twice for his anti-war activism.

To conquer fear
is the beginning
of wisdom.

BERTRAND RUSSELL

R. S. Thomas, born in Cardiff in 1913, was one of Wales's proudest voices and poets. He was a staunch nationalist, and his poetry, according to John Betjeman, will 'be remembered long after he is forgotten'. Thomas was nominated for a Nobel Prize in Literature in 1995 but lost out to Irish poet Seamus Heaney.

Mon Mam Cymbry.
That is, Anglesea is the
Mother of Wales.

THOMAS FULLER

Best-selling author **Ken Follett** was born in Cardiff in 1949 and began his career as a journalist for the *South Wales Echo*. His novel *Eye of the Needle* (1978) has sold over ten million copies, and one of his books, *The Pillars of the Earth* (1989), was on *The New York Times* Best Seller list for eighteen weeks!

Renowned and much-loved Welsh poet **Dannie Abse** (younger brother of Leo – see chapter headed 'We Can Be Heroes') was first published in 1949 and has been a Fellow of The Royal Society of Literature since 1983. In 1989, Abse received an honorary doctorate from the University of Wales.

Names are not always what they seem. The common Welsh name Bzjxxllwcp is pronounced Jackson.

MARK TWAIN

FOOD FOR THOUGHT

OUR LANDMARK DISHES

The **Welsh cake** is Wales's answer to the scone. Today we all know them as 'Welsh cakes' but before their popularisation throughout Wales, different regions knew them by different names, such as 'slashers' and 'wheel cakes'. Traditionally cooked on a bakestone, or griddle, these sugar-dusted cakes are flatter than your average English scone and are perfect as a treat any time of the day, but are best served as a lunchtime snack, perhaps when out walking the Beacons.

Laver bread, or Welshman's caviar as it is colloquially known, is one of Wales's signature foods. Dating back to the seventeenth century, laver bread is made from collected seaweed, which is boiled until soft and results in a black purée that has a high mineral content. Typically served as a breakfast dish with bacon and cockles – a result of another Welsh pastime, cockling.

Wales, though
small, cannot be
tidily parcelled.

TREVOR FISHLOCK

Wales has two national emblems – the leek and the daffodil. **Leek soup** tastes nicer than daffodil soup, hence why leek soup is a vital ingredient of Welsh national cuisine. A combination of leeks, potatoes, chicken broth and thick cream, it tastes of Wales – delicious. Serving suggestion: on a winter's day, when it's drizzly outside.

Tatws Pum Munud is a very Welsh stew. Smoked bacon, chicken stock, potatoes, onions, carrots and peas all cooked in a large frying pan until golden and served on a massive plate. Serve with thick, crusty doorstops of bread and butter to mop up the plethora of juices. Traditionally, the potatoes used in this dish are from leftover weekend roasties, so the potatoes are already cooked to a crisp – which means you can be eating this meal in under five minutes!

The English can have their crumpets, the Welsh have their **crempogs** – a fluffy take on the popular pancake. Self-raising flour, eggs, milk, salt and butter all whisked together and griddled and served with more butter. These Welsh pancakes are a traditional birthday treat, so next time your special day comes around order some of these and adorn them with your favourite toppings!

The Welsh are undoubtedly fond of their cheese and **Welsh rarebit** is the best example of this – a sauce of melted Cheddar poured sumptuously over toasted bread with a fried egg on top. The first recorded reference of this fondue-based dish was 'Welsh rabbit' in 1725, and while the origin of the name is shrouded in mystery, who cares when it's this tasty!

Wales isn't so
much a country
as a state of mind.

IFOR WILLIAMS

Cawl is widely considered to be the national dish of Wales, and for good reason too. This brilliant broth brings together lamb and leeks – two national heroes in one dish! – as well as potatoes, swede and carrots, all fused together in a thick stock. It's a perfect meal after a long day's tramping in the Welsh countryside!

Shepherd's pie – with lamb, not beef, obviously – has kept the Welsh well fed for centuries. You can add your own secret flavours, but the traditional Welsh ingredients are cooked lamb mince, onions and spices, covered in fluffy mashed potatoes with grilled cheese on top. Hearty and wholesome, and just what you need after a day of gambolling in the wild Welsh terrain.

Faggots have a long history in Wales. Traditionally made from pig's heart, liver, bacon and breadcrumbs, and minced together with herbs and served with gravy, mash and peas. In the middle ages, faggots were known as 'savoury ducks'. Sounds revolting, tastes anything but. At the beginning of the noughties the popular faggot-making company Mr Brains tried to create a National Faggot Week – it sadly failed to take off. But, no problem; you can enjoy them any day of the week anyway!

Glamorgan sausage is anything but meaty. This very Welsh dish is stuffed full of Caerphilly cheese, cooked leeks and breadcrumbs, bundled together sausage-style and then fried. Dating back to the 1800s, the Glamorgan sausage's popularity was revived during rationing in World War Two. The first printed reference to this famous sausage was in George Borrow's book, *Wild Wales*, in 1862.

The celebrated **Caerphilly cheese** originates from the town of that name in Mid Glamorgan. Crumbly and tangy, the taste is unmistakeable. The townsfolk of Caerphilly hold an annual three-day festival entitled The Big Cheese in July to honour it. In 2013, 80,000 Caerphilly-lovers turned up.

Roast lamb is, of course, synonymous with Welsh cuisine. The lamb is the National Animal of Wales and would be sacred if it weren't so tasty. Roast lamb with laver bread, served with buckets of mint sauce, is a Sunday afternoon tradition in Wales.

To be born in Wales… with music in your blood and with poetry in your soul, is a privilege indeed.

BRIAN HARRIS

MAPPING THE NATION

OUR WEATHER AND GEOGRAPHY

Wales's largest natural lake is **Bala Lake**, or Llyn Tegid, as it's called in Welsh. Located in Gwynedd, Bala Lake is 6.4 kilometres (4 miles) long, 1.6 kilometres (1 mile) wide, and covers an area of 11.4 square kilometres (4.4 square miles).

What I like about Wales is its closeness – not just its geography but also the friendliness of its people.

ED BAILEY

The longest river in Wales, the **Towy**, is
121 kilometres (75 miles) long and flows
down through the Cambrian Mountains
to Carmarthen Bay. On 28 July 1932,
local fisherman Alec Allen caught the
biggest freshwater fish up to that date,
with a rod and line, in the Towy. The fish,
a 176-kilogram (388-pound) sturgeon,
was over 2.7 metres (9 feet) in length.
According to local reports, a fisherman
on the opposite bank saw Mr Allen's
catch and was so terrified by its size
that he ran off screaming in terror!

Every mountain and stream,
every farm and little lane
announces to the World
that landscape is something
different in Wales.

R. S. THOMAS

The iconic **Snowdon** is the highest mountain summit in Wales, standing a proud 1,085 metres (3,560 feet) above sea level. Edmund Hillary used Snowdon as a 'training exercise' before conquering Mt Everest. From the top, on a clear day, you get a good view across Britain and Ireland: in fact, you should be able to spot twenty-four counties, twenty-nine lakes and seventeen islands!

I am proud to be Welsh because of our striking natural heritage. To me, Wales is just one big beautiful national park.

KIRSTY WILLIAMS

Snowdon's mammoth summit receives
the **highest rainfall** in Wales, with
approximately 4,572 millimetres
(180 inches) a year – or, put another
way, getting on for the height of
a giraffe! That's a lot of rain!

In the Bible, God made it rain for forty days and forty nights. That's a pretty good summer for Wales.

RHOD GILBERT

2 August 1990 was the day that Wales was basking in the **highest temperature** ever recorded in the country – 35.2 ºC (95.4 ºF) – at Hawarden Bridge in Flintshire. Coincidentally, within two weeks, 'Itsy Bitsy Teenie Weenie Yellow Polka Dot Bikini' by Bombalurina would be at the number one spot in the UK charts.

Lovely the woods, waters,
meadows, combes, vales,
All the air things wear that
build this world of Wales.

GERARD MANLEY HOPKINS

Wales's geography is beautiful, for sure. But did you know that its entire **land mass** covers just over 20,720 square kilometers (8,000 square miles) and measures 257 kilometres (160 miles) long by 97 kilometres (60 miles) wide. The entire Welsh coastline is 1,207 kilometres (750 miles) long – about a quarter of the length of the River Nile in Egypt.

The **Dale Peninsula** in south-west Pembrokeshire is the windiest part of Wales, with speeds of over 160 kilometres per hour (100 miles per hour) recorded. It's also the sunniest, with an annual average of over 1,800 hours – 4.9 hours a day on average. Not that sunny, actually.

Wales, Wales, sweet are thy
hills and vales,
Thy speech, thy song,
To thee belong,
O may they live ever in Wales.

EVAN JAMES

THE OBJECTS OF OUR DESIRE

ICONIC OBJECTS AND FAMOUS INVENTIONS

Every day when
I wake up,
I thank the Lord
I'm Welsh.

CERYS MATTHEWS

In 2010 a pair of Welshmen were named the world's best inventors. Robert Clarke and John Lockwood, from Gorseinon, Swansea, were crowned by the World Intellectual Property Organisation – the first time UK inventors have ever won. The pair had invented a groundbreaking new '**Sports Injury Rehabilitation Assistant**' (SIRA), the world's first digital stretching aid that helps sportspeople recover their strength after injury.

On 28 December 1888, Denbighshire-born
astronomer Isaac Roberts was the first to
take a clear, **deep-space 'photograph'**
of the Great Nebula of Andromeda
– now known as the Andromeda Galaxy
– and discovered its epic, if unexpected,
spiral shape. The Andromeda Galaxy
is 2.5 million light years from Earth.

Thy tongue makes Welsh as sweet as ditties highly penned, sung by a fair queen in a summer's bower, with ravishing division, to her lute.

WILLIAM SHAKESPEARE

Born in Usk in 1823, Alfred Russel Wallace was considered one of the greatest minds on evolutionary theory in the nineteenth century and also contributed to the **theory of natural selection through evolution**. A trusted friend of Englishman Charles Darwin, Wallace helped prompt the famed biologist into publishing his own findings in his groundbreaking *On the Origin of Species*, published in 1859, a year *later* than Wallace's own paper on natural selection theories.

While Colonel George Everest cannot stake any claim for inventing the world's tallest mountain, he will at least forever be associated with it. **Mount Everest** was named after the Crickhowell-born mountain surveyor by the Royal Geographical Society. Somewhat oddly, the mountain is not pronounced like Everest's own name, which is actually pronounced *Eve*-rest.

Edward George 'Taffy' Bowen, born
in Swansea in 1911, played a massive
part in the development of the **radar**
used during World War Two. Taffy's duty
was to design and build a transmitter
that would 'bounce' signals off objects
to determine their position. His work
contributed hugely to victory in the Battle
of Britain and the Battle of the Atlantic.

If you want someone to thank for working out your maths problems, Tenby-born Robert Recorde is your man. In 1557, Recorde invented the modern **equals sign** (=). He also introduced the **plus sign** (+) to Britain. Unsurprisingly, Recorde attended the University of Oxford at age thirteen.

If Robert Recorde's achievements
didn't = satisfaction, have no fear;
Welshman William Jones's achievements
will. Born in Anglesey in 1675,
mathematician Jones invented the
modern **symbol for the Greek pi** (ϖ)
in 1706. Here we go, 3.1459265359…

One of the best things to come from
Caerphilly (since the cheese) was the great
Tommy Cooper – he of the **red fez** and the
'Just like that!' catchphrase – and he was
a Welsh boy and proud. While he neither
invented magic nor comedy, Cooper did
invent putting them together – and even if
his tricks never worked and his jokes were
(deliberately) never very funny, somehow
the result was just magic. A legend.

To be honest, I think that I am a bit of a singer, coming from Wales; being Welsh, we are all very proud of our singing heritage.

IOAN GRUFFUDD

A LAW UNTO OURSELVES

THE PECULIAR LAWS THAT KEEP US OUT OF TROUBLE!

I feel privileged to be Welsh because our language, culture and sense of community give us a unique identity we are privileged to inherit.

RHYS MEIRION

Due to Sunday trading laws in the nineteenth century, pubs were shut across Wales, but a loophole in the act allowed travellers who had journeyed more than 3 miles to have an alcoholic drink.
(Surely you could just have lied to the barman about where you'd come from!)

No Welshman, or any person of Welsh
extraction or sympathies, of whatsoever
state or condition, [will] remain within
the walls of the said city [Chester]…
under pain of decapitation.

It makes me proud to
be Welsh when I see our
national flag flying high
above Caernarfon Castle. It
reminds me that we're still
here despite a lot of effort to
make us history.

TUDUR OWEN

It is illegal, under the Licensing Act 1872,
to be drunk on licensed premises,
e.g. a pub.

Thanks to the Town Police Clauses Act 1947,
a £1,000 fine awaits anyone who hangs
their clothes on a line across the street.

We've got the best scenery and landscape in the world, our own language, culture, history.

LLINOS LEE

Under the Currency and Banknotes
Act 1928, it is an offence to destroy
or deface a banknote by printing,
stamping or writing on it.
(But why would you want to
destroy money anyway?)

Under the Madhouses Act 1774 it is an offence to keep 'more than one Lunatick' without having a licence for 'a madhouse'.

Old Sunday trading laws meant that 'transactions for the purposes of which a shop may be open in England and Wales for the serving of customers on Sunday' included 'meals or refreshments whether or not for consumption at the shop at which they are sold, but not including the sale of fried fish and chips at a fried fish and chip shop'. So, it was illegal for a British traditional fish and chip shop to open on a Sunday but not for a Chinese takeaway to do so (and they could sell fish and chips).

Despite the British government slashing
45,000 laws from the statute book
in 2006, it is still, under the Salmon
Act 1986, illegal to 'handle salmon
in suspicious circumstances'.

The Library Offences Act 1898 banned all gambling in libraries. (There must have been a lot of gambling in libraries!)

Under the Easter Act 1928, Easter Sunday should be fixed as the first Sunday after the second Saturday in April. (Hard to believe though it is, this law never really took off.)

Following the historic devolution of 1988, the National Assembly for Wales passed the first ever Welsh parliamentary act into law on 12 November 2012. The law in question was the National Assembly for Wales (Official Languages) Bill, which recognised that both Welsh and English would be the official languages of the nation's assembly meetings.

Under the Tax Avoidance Schemes
Regulations 2006, it is illegal not to tell
the taxman anything you do not want
him to know, but legal not to tell him
information you do not mind him knowing.
(Confused?)

Under the Wildlife and Countryside
Act 1981, it is illegal to eat mute
swan (it's a protected species) unless
you're the Queen of Great Britain.

Under the Licensing Act 1872, it is an offence to be 'drunk in charge of a carriage, horse, cow or steam engine, whilst in possession of a loaded firearm.'(Drunk in possession of a cow? Sounds fun.)

What is this life if, full of care,
We have no time to
stand and stare?

W. H. DAVIES

THERE'S NO PLACE LIKE HOME

FAMOUS PLACES TO SEE AND THINGS TO DO

The **World Alternative Games**, held in September at Llanwrtyd Wells, Powys, is a Welsh delight to be proud of. They showcase the world's wackiest 'sports' with anything-but-typical events, which include Bog Snorkelling, the Man versus Horse Marathon and the Real Ale Wobble, as well as bale-throwing, stone-skimming, pea-shooting, egg-throwing and wife-carrying championships. Sign up now for a slice of quintessential Welsh fun!

I always think of us as a community, rather than a country. No matter where Welsh people live throughout the UK, we help and look out for each other.

BRYN WILLIAMS

With fifty-seven letters in its name, pronouncing the town of **Llanfairpwllgwyngyllgogerychwymdrobwllllanty siliogogogoch**, Anglesey, is more of a mouthful than the entire Abergavenny Food Festival! Meaning 'St Mary's Church in the hallow of the white hazel near a rapid whirlpool and the Church of St Tysilio of the red cave', it's well worth a visit to this town just to get a photo in front of Europe's longest place name.

From Brecon to Cardiff Bay, the **Taff Trail** is an 88-kilometre-long (55-mile-long), off-road tourist trek that takes in many of the country's leading archaeological wonders, pre-industrial towns and the beautiful moorlands of the Brecon Beacons. Every September, hundreds of cyclists take on the gruelling Taff Trail Cycle Challenge, and the first one to the end of the trail receives a hero's welcome – all for a good cause, of course. This event has become one of the most anticipated on the summer calendar. Join in – if you dare!

Portmeirion is a slice of Italy in north Wales. Built in the style of a Mediterranean village, Portmeirion is full of exotic wonders that will confuse your eyes. Take a trip to this Gwynedd wonder and absorb an eyeful of the strange architecture of Sir Bertram Clough Williams-Ellis's designs, including Central Piazza, Hercules Gazebo and Unicorn Cottage – all playful and entertaining structures that you won't see anywhere else in Great Britain.

Among our ancient mountains,
And from our lovely vales,
Oh, let the prayer re-echo:
'God bless the
Prince of Wales!'

GEORGE LINLEY

Recently voted Britain's greatest natural wonder, the **Dan-yr-Ogof caves** – situated within the Brecon Beacons National Park – form the largest cave system in western Europe. Every year thousands of people arrive eager to view the stalagmites and stalactites. In 1912 the Morgan brothers, who owned the land, were the first to explore parts of the caves that for thousands of years had been home to ancient remains of human ancestors. Still not fully discovered, many experts believe there could be as many as 160 kilometres (100 miles) of caves yet to explore. If you go, make sure you take a torch!

Swansea's **Mumbles Mile** is Wales's best-known, and world-famous, pub crawl. Taking in nine pubs on the 2-mile-long, sea-facing Mumbles Road, the challenge is to drink a pint at each pub before moving on – whoever makes it to the end is crowned the victor (or victors). Dylan Thomas could often be found propping up the bar in The Antelope (which is still there to this day), before moving on down the road to another one of his favourite joints, The Mermaid (sadly since lost in a fire), once famously described by him as 'my Mumbles Mermaid'.

Close to the westernmost point of the country you'll find the historic and quaint **St David's** – Britain's smallest city. With a population of mere thousands its city status, having been abolished in 1888, was reinstated in by the Queen in 1994. William the Conqueror had also paid a visit during his historic pilgrimage of 1081.

With fourteen separate 'obstacles for intruders' – including murder holes, arrow slits and drawbridges – **Beaumaris Castle**, Anglesey, is a fourteenth-century military marvel and was once a state-of-the-art fortress. Started by Edward I in 1295, the design of its famous concentric 'walls within walls', a first of its kind, took thirty-five years to complete.

The beautiful seafront location of Llandudno is famous for something other than its beaches. In 1860, it saw the arrival of the first **Punch & Judy show**. One hundred and fifty years later, and three times a day from Easter to September, the 35-minute show is still put on by the Codman family, who still use the same oak puppets first used by their ancestor Richard Codman, the creator of one of history's favourite quarrelling couples.

In 2013, **Rhossili beach**, off Mumbles Head, was named by TripAdvisor as the best beach in the UK and the third best in Europe! It's also home to the historic shipwreck of the *Helvetia*, a Norwegian ship that got stuck in the sand on 1 November 1887. You can still see the ribs of the ship's hull poking up, but perhaps not for much longer. With each passing day, the Atlantic Ocean claims back a little bit more of the wreck.

But it is my
happiness to be
half Welsh, and
that the better half.

AMY URIELL

If you're interested in finding out more about our books, find us on Facebook at **Summersdale Publishers** and follow us on Twitter at **@Summersdale**.

www.summersdale.com